The Quiet Lion

By Aspen M. Laboy

All rights reserved. No part of this book may be produced in any manner whatsoever without written permission from the publisher, except in the case of brief quotations embodied in critical articles and reviews.

The author expresses great gratitude to those who have contributed, whatever it may be, to previous, present, and forthcoming books.

Copyright ©2018 by Aspen M. Laboy
ISBN: 978-0-692-08526-4
First Edition

Inside art and cover art by Calvin Banks

"The Quiet Lion reads as if Aspen is a stream of thought, directly from the collective conscious of humanity. Her symbolic and introspective writings are a doorway to explore your deeper emotions and find your spiritual identity."
- Maurice Bailey

"I first encountered Aspen in my English Comp. I class at Metropolitan Community College. Her writing was fresh and clear and reached out to the reader tenderly and insightfully. These poems continue that clarity and humanity asking the questions that we all seek answers to. Some sparkle, some flow gently like tears, some roar, and some laugh with the wisdom of joy beyond her years. These poems share a thoughtful and quiet strength of spirit with confidence and grace."
- Bud Cassiday

"Aspen Laboy's poems are careful totems of spirit and insight, little darts of truth both sensitive and sharp, which always find their mark. It's kind of amazing how much she can capture in so few words, asking us all to explore the question, 'do I dare/anticipate/the world/while it/disintegrates?'"
- Jeff Lacey

For those who question the answers they seek.

Fear

Don't let the lion in, but
don't let it out either.
Its claws are sharp,
its ears can hear,
its teeth are sharp,
its eyes are near . . .

The Quiet Lion

Sitting
in this chair
I write
this song
for you
and all
them too.
Do not
whisper
anymore,
your back
is runnin'
out the door.
Look back
because
you don't

want more,
you'll want it
more than
ever before.
The jukebox
sings and
angels ring.
Beyond
the sound
he watches,
waiting.
The crystal globe
can only take
so much heat
to explode.

Camels

Will we become
a wasteland
or
will we die
from secondhand
smoke?
Choking
on the ashes
of
harsh reality.
Provoking
God,
when will we
stop?
Mentality,
the seed of
creation.
Free us from
destruction.
Put on
a production.
Lead us
not into
temptation.
Show me
love
and
divination.
Differentiate
discrimination.
Free will
is not
willingly free,
between
you and me.

Love God, Love Woman

Your hands
created
us.
Our hands
created
other things,
but have
destroyed
much more.

Your hands
touch
me.
Our hands
touch
each other,
and will
create
much more.

Growing

Again, comes
savage winds
and
malicious rain.

Oil drips
make light again.

Devils dwell
in stumps
of trees.

No one knows
and
no one sees.

Spring will bring
the birth
of news.

Indestructible
wooden pews.

Wo(man)

micro waves
caress
my brain
whispers
of
comfort and pain
seduce me
morality
and
temptation
is the only
complication
or is it,
me?

the cursed creation

Angels

I wish I was
an angel.
Something greater
than just
good.
Being human
is exhausting,
mesmerizing,
a curse.
For the love of
my universe,
please,
let me
be
free!
Irony
Hypocrisy
Selfishness
Suicide
Satan
will not overcome,
will not overcome,
will not overcome.
I will be
Imperishable.

The Prophecy

Rebel
from
society.

Repel
the
hate.

Re-tell
the
story.

Reveal
the
gate.

The Counsel

I am coming . . .

Here I am,
I am here,
am I here?

Are you here?

Here you are,
you are here
now.

Armageddon

I

All the stars
are falling
and the flames
are rising.

I don't know
why
I just keep crying.

The government
just keeps on
lying.

The firmament is
slowly
dying

God,
where art thou?

II

Burn the paper
of the savior
and feel
the wrath
of
God and Satan.

The time is now
or
the time is never,
but somehow
time goes on
forever.

Turn the pages,
read the book.

You will find
the answer,
look.

III

The love
that we share
is always
true.

Tainted faith
is always
false.

Light will shine
in every corner.

Darkness
scatters
chaotic
disorder.

Should I care
that you don't?
Do I blink
with both eyes?
Does the third
cleanse itself?
Is there room
for another book
on the shelf?
How does one
love
when they hate?
How do two love
when one hates?
Do I dare
anticipate
the world
while it
disintegrates?

IV

don't let them
do it
don't let them
win

you are strong

you know

what to do

before they
do it

think of this

was there ever

any bliss?

V

Man,
you are truly
evil.

You come
to me
a poisonous needle.

I devour you,

then share
with you.

You should not
have offered in
the first place.

I should have walked away.

VI

I don't know

why

he has to be

that way.

I do know

why

I have to be

this way.

To keep him

away.

VII

In the beginning
is where
we started.

In the end
we are somewhat
parted.

Each day
feels like
a thousand years.

A thousand years
feels like
one day.

Now

Death is
so sudden
and so
common
these days.

The life
all around
stays the same
but will change.

The path
that you take
are the rules
of the game.

The moments
in time
are becoming
today.

Purpose

I realize
what I am
doing now.

I am here
for
a reason
someway,
somehow.

You will
notice everything
you do.

You will
notice all
the others too.

I hope
you will realize
one day
too.

Visions

Ancient calls
awaken
the quiet sand.

The river slithers,
a snake
within the land.

The sun,
beautiful
rising
light.

The dawn
kills
the hopeless night.

Good Luck

Buddha belly
Four-leaf clover
Heads-up penny
Cliffs of Dover

Rabbits foot
Pot of gold
Cri-kee the cricket
The wise are old

Double rainbow
Leprechaun
Number seven
Break of dawn

Wheel of fortune
Wishbone
The North Star
Jade stone

Truth Pt. II

The blunt
and bottle
are my knives.

Everyday
it gets harder
to cry.

There is a fungus
that grows
on rye.

Pay attention
to truth
and lies.

The leaves
are starting
to fly,
then later
they all just
die,

but do not worry,

they all
come back
again.

The question is
just why?

The Quiet Lion

I'm ahead of
the time,
makin' rhythms
and rhymes.

Ain't no gold
on my mind,
only truth
and no lies.

You can try,
you can
really try.

Then you wonder,
why you so
low
to the ground?

Look around,
keep your head
up, not down.

Be proud
of yourself.

Is it the end
or the beginning?

Do I dare
discover?

Do I care
enough?

It looks like
Lucifer's winning,

but there is
always
a good ending,

or is it the beginning?

Aspen Monet Laboy was born and raised in Omaha, Nebraska. She currently attends Metropolitan Community College and plans to achieve an Associate of Arts degree. From childhood, Aspen has enjoyed and experienced other mediums of art such as music, photography, painting and drawing. Her previous and first poetry book titled "Spirit" was published in March of 2017.

aspenmlaboy.tumblr.com

Maurice Bailey: Audio Producer, at Maurice Bailey Productions LLC

Calvin Banks: Art Teacher, Ralston High School

Bud Cassiday: English Instructor, Metropolitan Community College

Jeff Lacey: English Instructor, Ralston High School

www.ingramcontent.com/pod-product-compliance
Lightning Source LLC
Chambersburg PA
CBHW032109040426
42449CB00007B/1231